something here to see

g h anonymous

SOMETHING HERE TO SEE

published by IPBooks, Queens, NY

ISBN: 978-1-956864-51-9

dedicated to my family

&

Mary
Paula
Joanie
Carolina
Christine

&

Jack

^
(*_*)

each of us will recall
our first experiences
with our first iPhone

like being tossed in a pool
we learned to swim

I pondered what kind of mind
invented this amazing little gadget
that contains our lives

Pictures Memories and Musings
destined to be choreographed
and bound together to be shared

thus began the interplay
of errors and trials
that evolved to form
this MiniTome

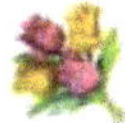

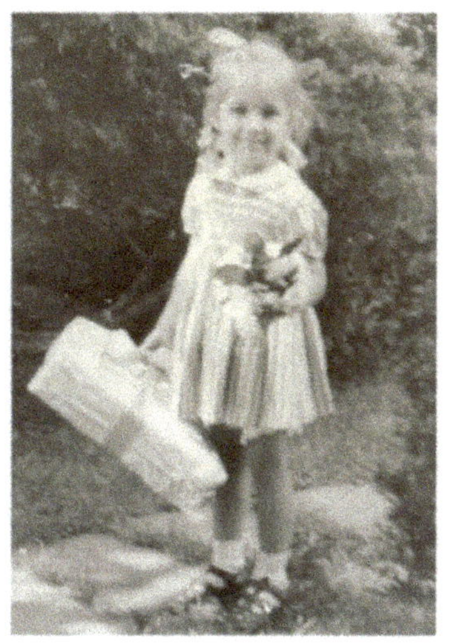

What is a present ?
a gift
a was
an is
a will be
a now

Inspiration...in your words

"So let me start"...

There were nail holes
you could touch
some large and deep
some small
barely discernible

They attest to a community
destroyed
to irreversible loss
of life
of creative force

Like the mezuzahs
they are gone
we know they were
by the holes
left behind

Re: Inspirational...in your own words...

That is so moving
So moving

ca. 1945

A NUTCRACKER SUITE

♫ Hop hoppity hop hop
hop hop hop...

(the Persian rug
suggests the choreography)

♫ ...a jump a jump
a jump a jump
a jump a jump a jump (boom)

(leap to touch the chandelier)

♫ ...te dum de dum
de dum de dum
de dum te dum te dum (DUM!)

(gallop between the windows
at opposite ends of the room)

IMPROVISE
until the Victrola needs
to be recranked

Bellum
redundans

amare
vixet

exclamavit
conatus detessus
dormivit

ineptum
flevit

terminus ligatum
omnis mortuus est

^
War
redundant

love
lived

cried
tried   tired
slept

inept
wept

ends tied
all died
~

^

Guerre
redondant

aimé(e)
vivait

crié
essayé   fatigué
dormi

fiables
pleurer

extrémités liées
tous morts

~

^
Krieg
überflüssig

Liebe
lebte

schrei
versucht   müde
schlaf

hilflos
weinen

zusammengebunden
alle sterben
~

^
Mlkhmh
iberik

libe
gelebt

geshrign
gefrauvt   mid
geshlafn

shvakh
geveynt

ends teyd
ale geshtarbn
~

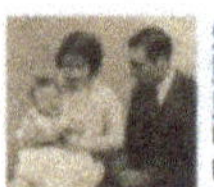

Queen Elizabeth II; Queen Elizabeth, the Queen Mother; King George VI
by Marcus Adams
bromide print, 2 December 1926
NPG P140(8)

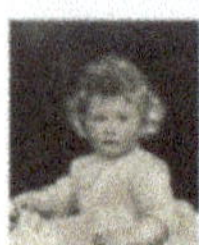

Queen Elizabeth II
by Marcus Adams
bromide print, June 1927
NPG P140(18)

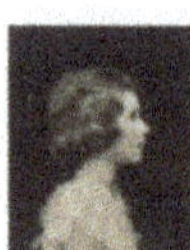

Queen Elizabeth II
by Marcus Adams
bromide print, February 1939
NPG P140(20)

when I was born

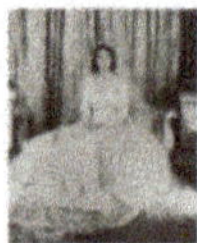

Queen Elizabeth II
by Baron Studios
bromide print, 20 November 1947
NPG P1416

when I was 7

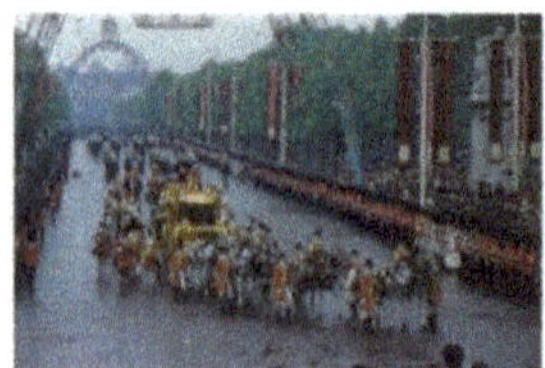

when I was 13

"MEMORY IN TRANSLATION"

als ich war zehn
hatte ich eine Erinnerung
eine Erinnerung
zu erinnern
spater

spater
ist
jetzt

when I was ten
I had a memory
a memory
to remember
later

later
is
now

quand j'avais dix ans
j'avais un souvenir
un souvenir
a souvenir
plus tard

plus tard
c'est
maintenant

to be

free

to sing
a song

of love

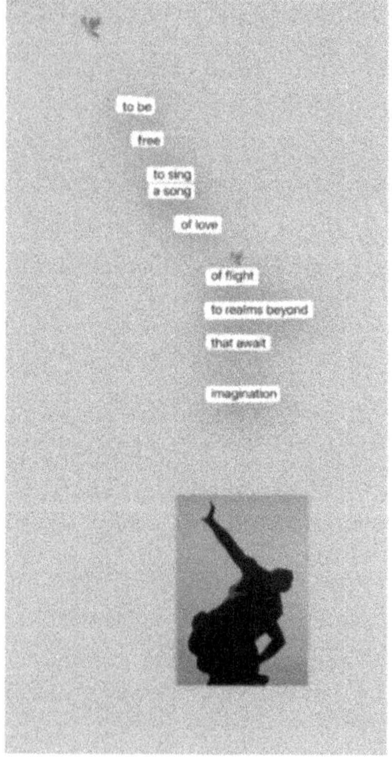

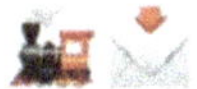

思想思想思想

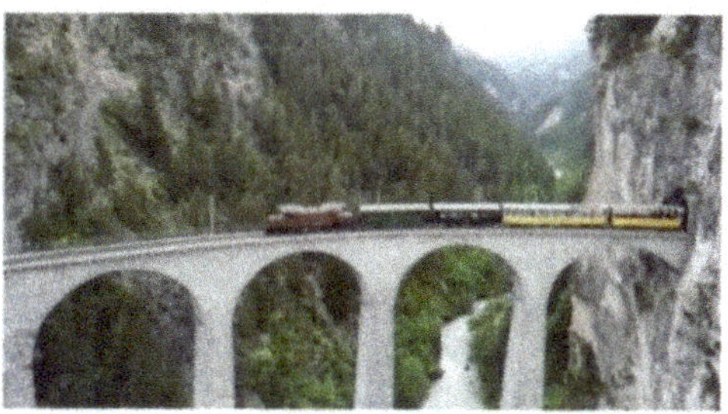

....train.........................of thought....

"So, say whatever goes through your mind. Act as though, for instance, you were a traveller sitting next to the window of a railroad carriage and describing to someone inside the carriage the changing views that you see outside... " (Freud, 1917, p.235).

⏳

Our Hour

lean and mean
means and dreams
ends and means
means extremes

outside out
inside in
inside out
outside in

outside seems
inside seen
seem extreme
inside dreams

might in sight
left or right
left and right
right insight

once was where
where there was then
there was when
twice five meant ten

Our Hour

went and spent   ($ for dreams)
left with scent   (pheromones)
dreamt and dreamt   (unintelligible)
no intent   (without context)

outside road   (a path)
inside rode   (driven)
visual code   (imagination)
rode that mode   (along for the ride)

was it real   (reality)
it was reel   (like a movie)
it was real   (of a movie)
reel in reel   (picture in picture)

what are memes   (knowledge)
dreams with seams   (repressed)
reseen scenes   (assembled)
dreams in dreams   (resurfacing)

mean as steel   (analysis is difficult)
means to heel   (intended to bind)
see a wheel   (hope in time)
meant to heal   (to release)

in
the
guest room
in Opa's house
I appear to myself
sitting on the floor
facing myself
manipulating an iridium rod

there has been a silent explosion
debris is suspended in a cloud
that if reconstructed
could be painted

the ⚔ is
phosphorescent
👁   👁

mouth
👅
to
hand
and back
✋ back and forth ✋
taste inspect ❤ taste
inspect wave shake rotate
taste shake · wave inspect
"tap" "tap tap" "taptaptap"
"BANG"! "BANG BANG"!!

"SHRIEK"

💤

(repeat)

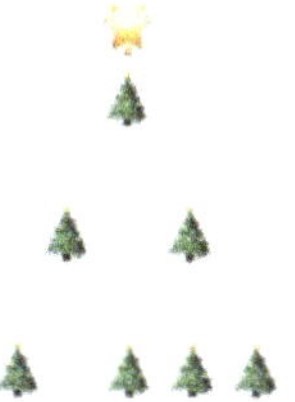

One go-round
on a merry-go-round
was more than enough for me

Time to see
what what will be

one more round
on the merry-go-round

Money will be
for each to see

one more go-round
on the merry-go-round

A Christmas Tree
for all to see

go round and round
on the Merry-Go-Round

Arcadian Dream

I dream
I am in the guest room
in my Grandmother's House

the room has three exposures

the south window overlooks my
Arcadian Garden

a meandering cinder path
contains random fruit trees
and a row of boxed hydrangea
bushes

mysteriously

some years pink

some years blue

centered

an oval Garden of Roses
(infested with iridescent beetles)

at the epicenter

a reimagined fountain

downstairs

in a pantry cabinet

a "flit-can" is prepared

to spray
poison

at the garden insects

beyond the path

a pair of bemused Stone Ladies

larger than life

guard a pergola
with an unremarkable floor

it was fun to paint them
with water
on a hot summer day

in Springtime

an umbrella of leaves
burst from vines
entwined
invisible in winter
to enclose a Pavilion

from early morning

late into night

at varying intervals

shrieks pierce the air

as humans

on the Giant Cyclone Ride

thrill

to terrifying

plunges

at Palisades Amusement Park

between the pergola and the park
lived one Albert Anastasia

he was murdered in a barber's chair
around the corner
from my ballet class
in Carnegie Hall

an aerial photograph
featured his mansion
on the front page
of the Daily News

"Ja"

"und ich habe gedacht er war a
Gentleman"
my grandmother remarked

occasionally
she had chatted with his brother
through the chain-link fence
that separated us from them

"his brother is a Priest"
she added

to the East

beyond the garden

stood an ancient willow tree

below

the Hudson River
with it's haunting hooting ferries

flowed seaward
under the mighty
George Washington Bridge

past a Little Red Lighthouse

soon to be the title
of a bestselling children's book

one Fall

the magnificent Weeping Willow
was uprooted in a hurricane

never to be replaced

at Dusk

 a fox continued to
appear
 as if the beloved tree

were still there

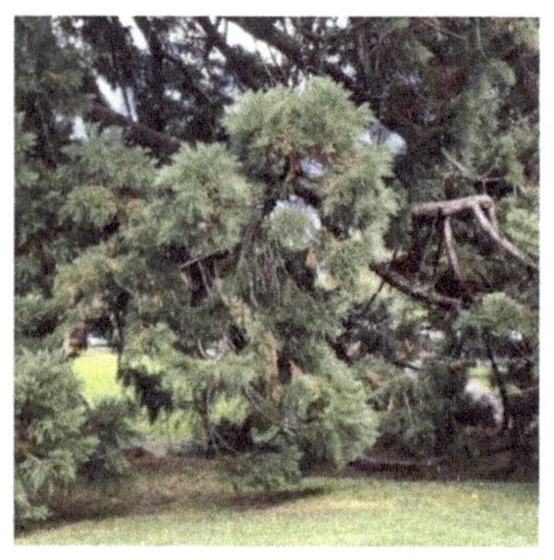

A local habitation and a name.
Some tricks hath strong
        imagination,
That if it would but apprehend
        some joy;
It comprehends some bringer of
        that joy;
Or in the night, imagining some fear,
How easy is a bush supposed
        a bear!

(A Midsummer Night's Dream, 5.1)

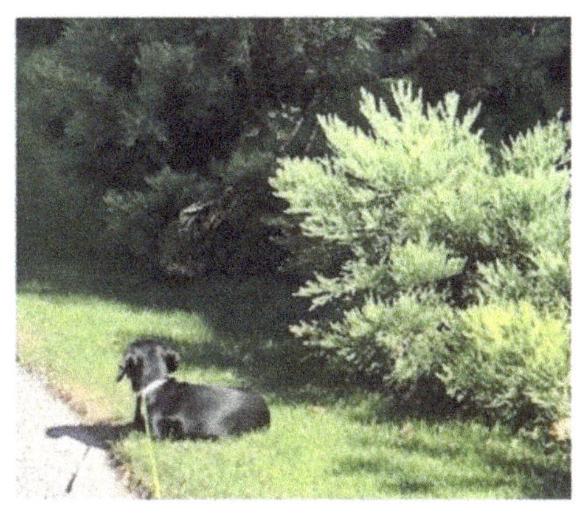

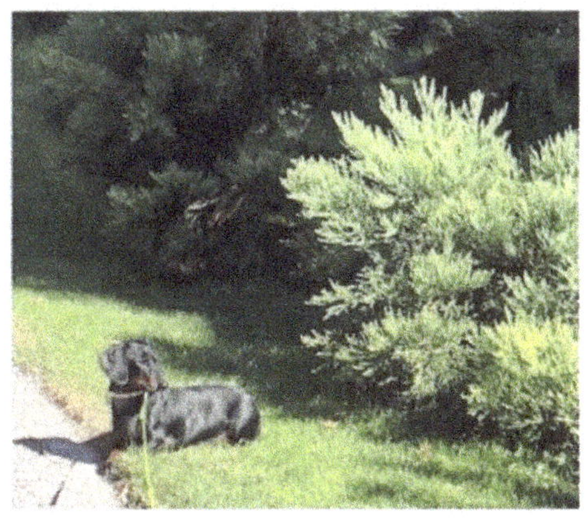

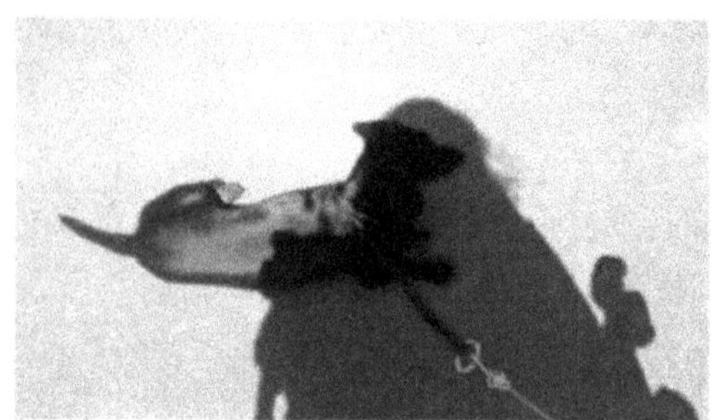

Quote for Today

"Until one has loved an animal a
part of one soul has remained
unawakened "

Anatole France

Quote for Today

"If the path be beautiful let us not ask where it leads "

Anatole France

Re: Quote for today

"If you don't know where you are going, you'll end up someplace else".

Yogi Berra

Re: Quote for today

Better than Anatole France

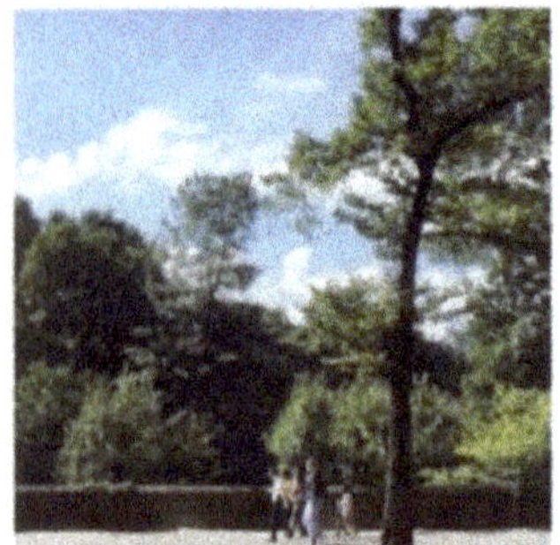

after

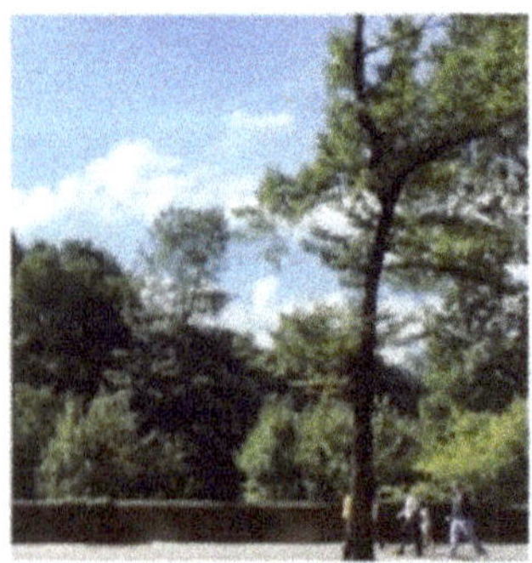

before

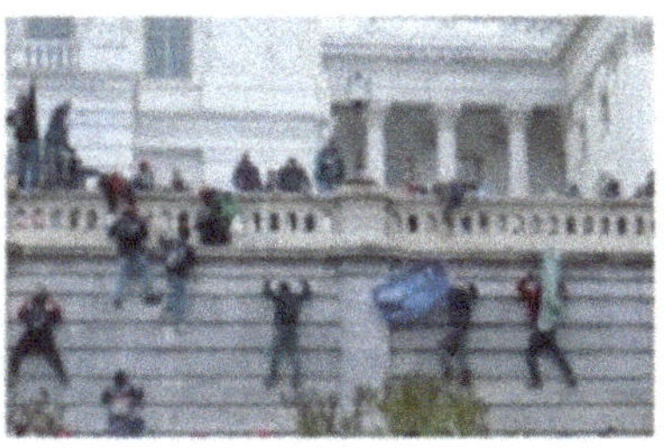

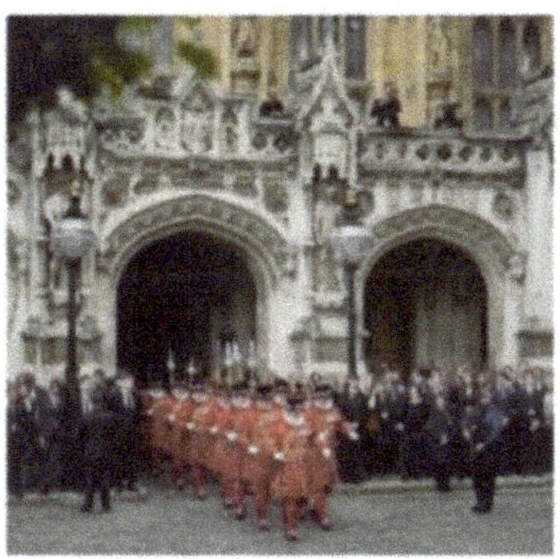

'Sedition'

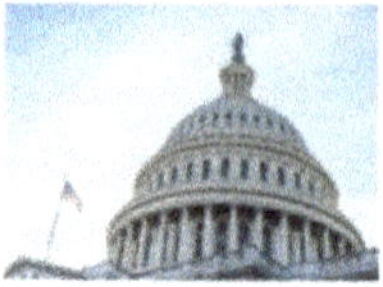

CAPITOL
stairs
stairs stairs
stairs crowd stairs
stairs crowd crowd stairs
crowds crowds crowds crowds

wait
wait
wait
wait
wait
wait
wait
wait
wait

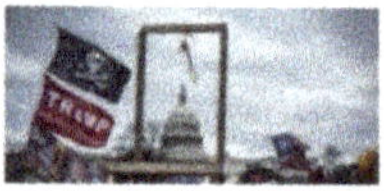

wait
wait
wait
wait
wait
wait
wait
wait
wait

crowds crowds crowds crowds
stairs crowd crowd stairs
stairs crowd stairs
stairs stairs
stairs
CAPITOL

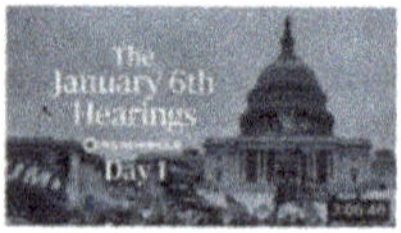

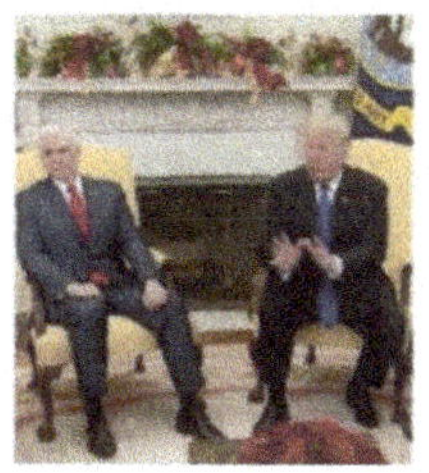

 "It's common sense
to hang Mike Pence"
thought Trump one winter day

he planned for that
with shit and shat
and flags on flying display

do not forget
your MAGA hat
to prove you're here to play

at "army man"
or "shaman beast"
no matter what they say

"go make it zilch"
what minds have built
but law got in the way

now all those jerks
acquire perks
in jails quite far away

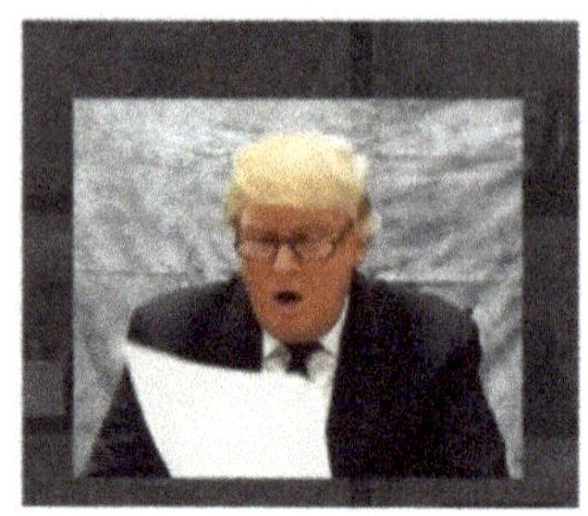

Dilemma

'tis a proffer
might he wish
to wish unwish
can not

attatched provision
he might wish
not to wish
and not

language crafted
wish confessed
might confess
but not

contract breached
confessed to breach
might rebreach
or not

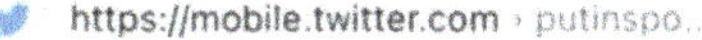

Trump Is Putin's Poodle

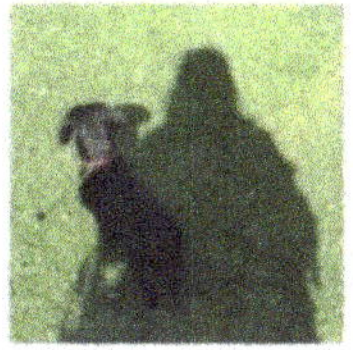

"sit"

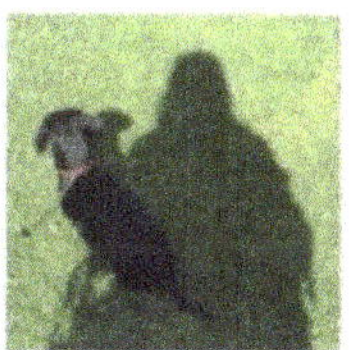

Those who know poodles can see that Trump's a different breed

BLANK UNIVERSE

marks
and sounds
signify
identification
with ideation

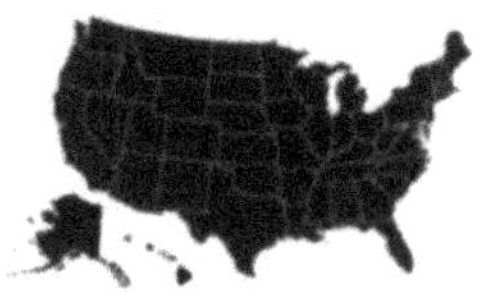

It was black ...

sound of pain

ending a beginning
beginning an ending

pain of sound

... it was black.

Subject: 🍦 Ice Cream Dream

"I WANT I SCREAM"

"I WANT ICE CREAM"

reality
fantasy

memoir
fiction

science
fiction

friction
fiction

---

open 👁s
hearing 👂s
helping ✋s
healing ❤️s

U B ME ?

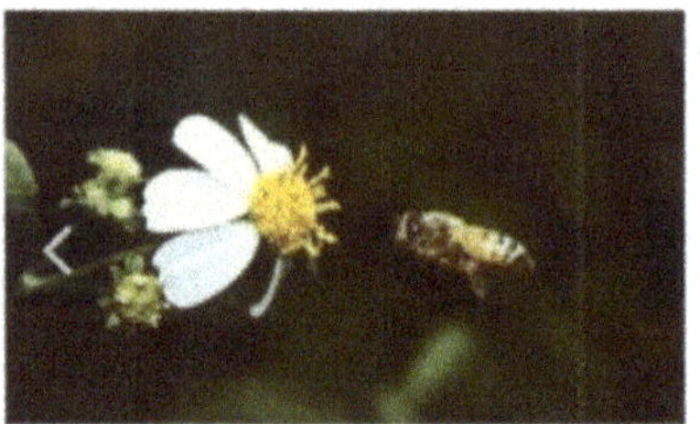

From whence came zero?
conundrum about nothing

INKBLOT

Adam | Eve

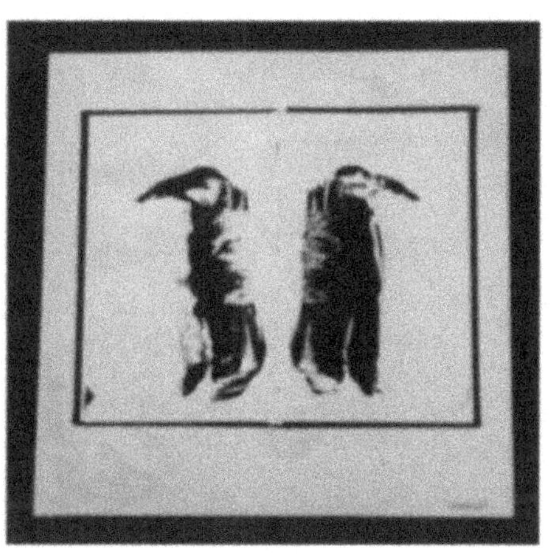

School Figures

Zen
predawn
daily

silent sounds
of blades
cutting ice

thoughts preconscious
music memorized
present to mind

Sometimes someone put on a
record.

lyrics impressed
misremembered

"When you walk through a storm
 keep your head up high
 and don't be afraid of the dawn
 at the end of the sky
 theres a golden dream
 and the sweet silver song of a lark"

   ♫ "walk on
      walk on
      with hope in your heart
      and you"ll never walk alone
      you'll never walk alone"

"CAROUSEL"
lyrics by Rogers and Hammerstein

⛸

Alone

centered in a universe of ice
terrified

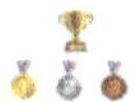
"Princess Aurora"

Dum dum dum DaDa dum .....
♫ ♫ ♫ ♫ ♫ ♫ ♫ ♫ ♫ ♫ ♫ ♫

It matters what you did.
Judges will opine.

🏆
🥇 🥈 🥉

This you will do again
            again and
            again and again
                and again
🔑

DISCIPLINE
self discipline

CRITICISM
self criticism

REFLECTION

PRESENCE OF MIND

SCRABBLE BABBLE

first word:

Y
A
P

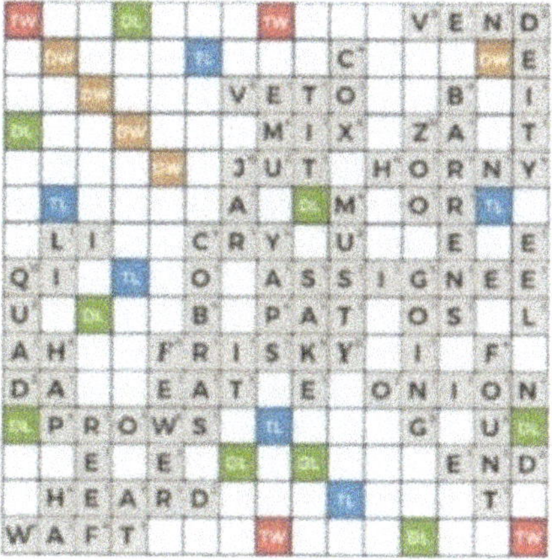

last letter: I

last words:

```
  T
M I X
  T
```

we were in business

Ned had a wagon

he rented it to me in exchange for a
commission on potholders I made
with a craft kit

we also sold crabs

we caught them off of a neighbor's
dock and dragged them around the
neighborhood in a bucket half filled
with the water in which they had once
lived free

sometimes one of the neighbors
bought one or two (if available)

it did not occur to us to wonder what
happened to them

we were not allowed in each others'
houses

my house had a deep outside porch

on rainy days we played cards
WAR with 2 decks
that could last for days

other days focused on civil
engineering

my driveway
was a thick bed
of opaque tumbled stones
scattered unbound
into the grass

the stones in Ned's driveway
were contained
rough and gray
called gravel

we had toy plastic hoes
suitable for creating roads
and parking lots
in destinations imagined

a bank (box) here

a school (shoebox) there

the train station way over there

Ned shared his vehicles

on Fridays
we erased our projects with a large
broom and restored the driveway
to repose

Fathers returned on weekends
play resumed on Mondays

Ned had a temper
I did not

towards summer's end
we had a fight

the center of the rustic road
that separated our realms
was negotiated
and defined by a line of white chalk
procured from a location
somewhere in Ned's house

there were no weapons

the war was short
less than a day

soon summer would end by default

~~~~~
~~~~~

the sunroom
in my Grandmothers house
overlooked New York City

I wondered
where in the mass of gray buildings
(so miniature in the distance)
Ned was

~~~~~

when summer returned
Ned was 8
I was 9
~~~~~

🎵 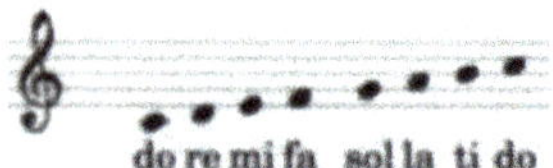 dreams

I am who I am

you are who you are

he
she   are what they are
it

we are who you are

you are who they are

are they who I am?

Re: 

I am the walrus

Sent from my iPhone

Walrus and the Carpenter

Am I Alice?

Yes

🎵🌈 dreams

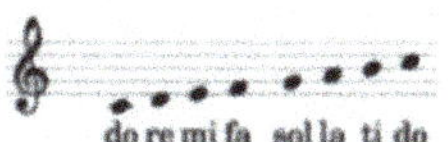

📝 Reverie

we were in business

Ned had a wagon

Wonderland

if I am Alice
and you are The Walrus
could a walrus also be Ned?

Related Maps

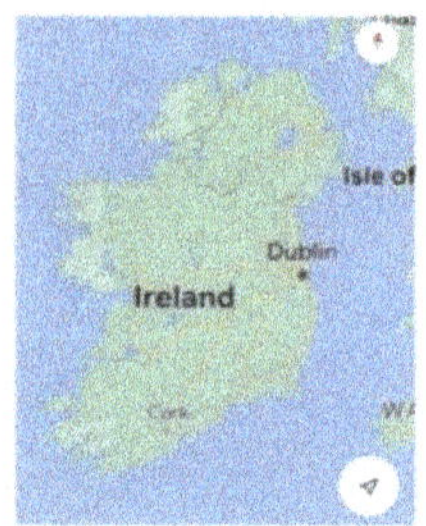

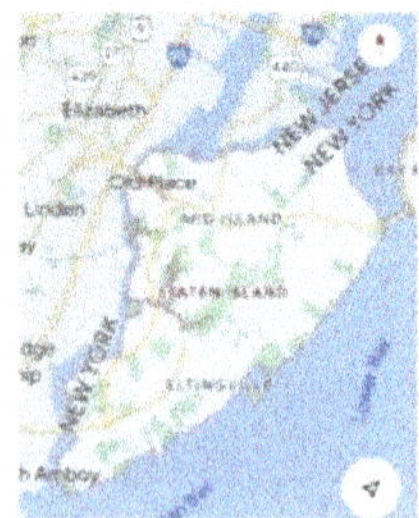

Where am I ?

D835
Yavuzeli
D850
D400
Sam
Beykent
Bilek
Gaziantep
D400
Oğuzeli

Turkey
aray
Malatya
Kahramanmaraş
Adana
Gaziantep
Mersin
Antakya
Syria

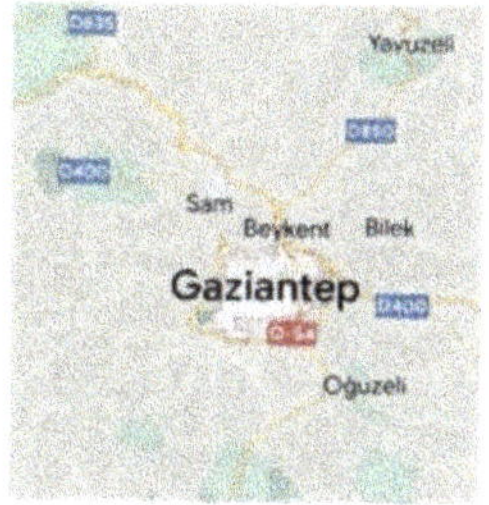

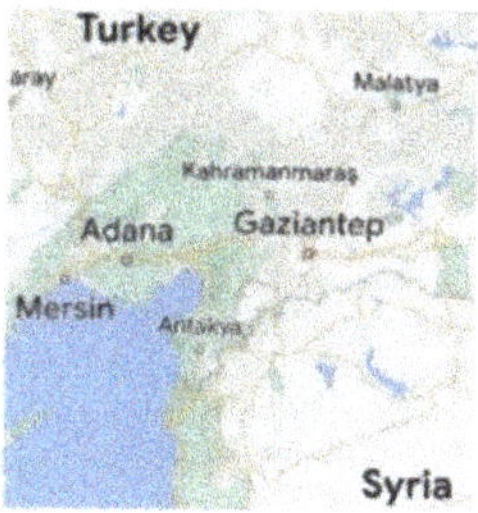

Earthquake ❗

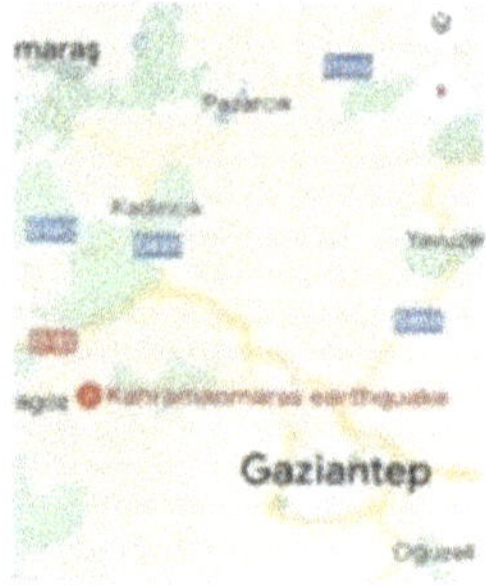

More than 4,000 killed in Turkey, Syria after powerful earthquake and aftershocks

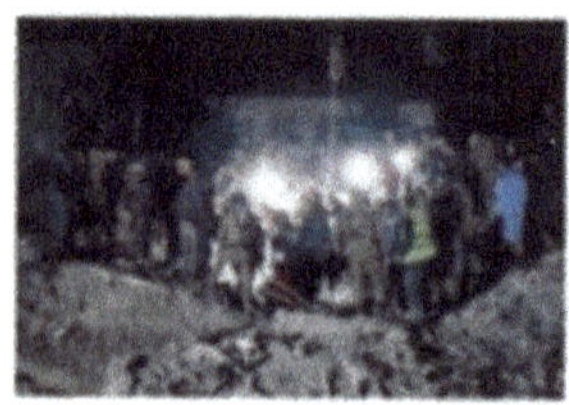

2022 "Gone Tomorrow"

Here Today
  still alive
  ...an old Pope died
  🎵 "Everlasting Handmaids Sing"

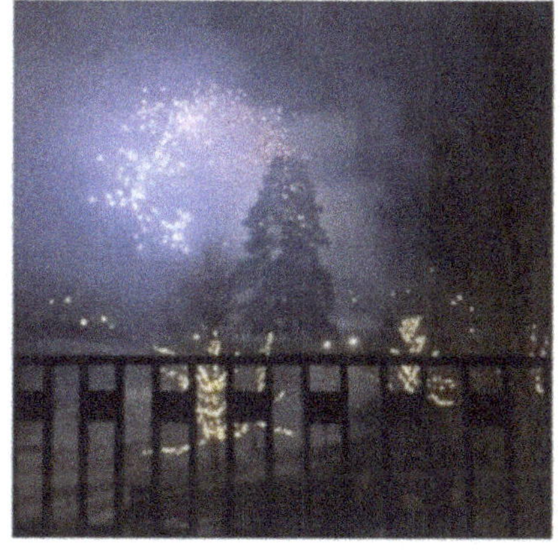

There Tomorrow
  nightmare weary
  ...almost clearly
  📚 "Tales re-told begin again"

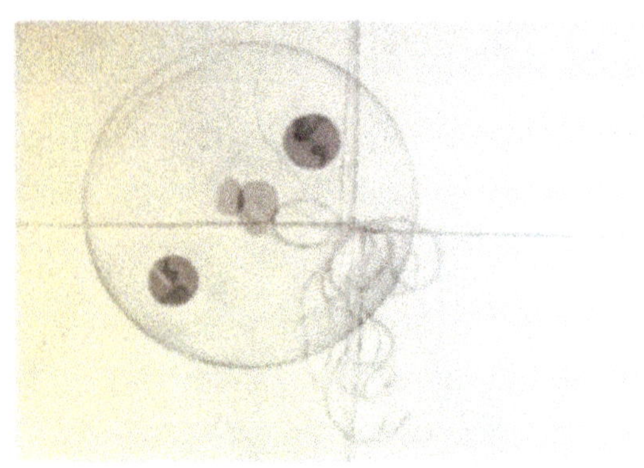

container for earth

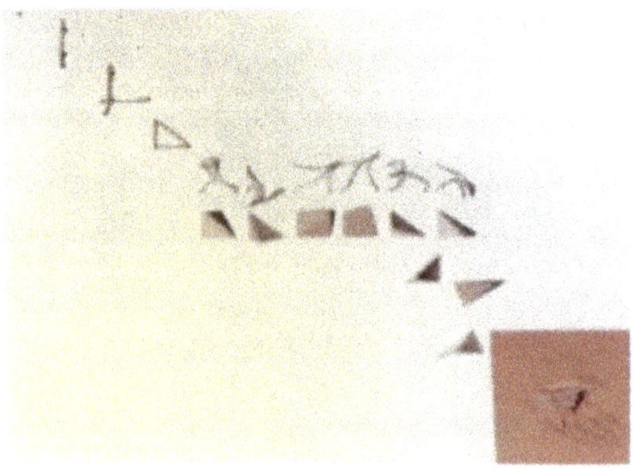

what is architecture?

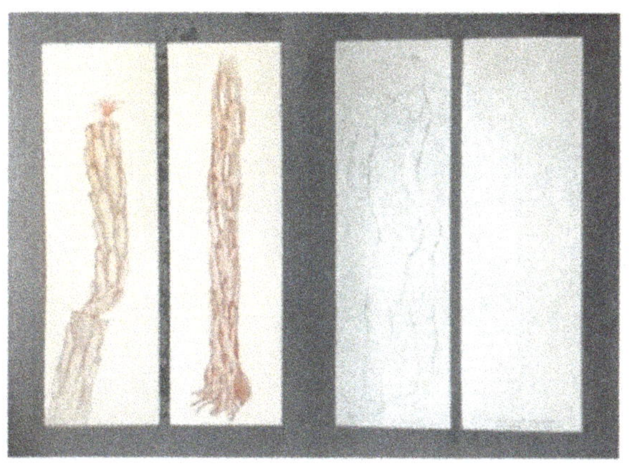

eros   thanatos

📞 "Eisenman's Bakery"
"Which crumb do you want"?

Once upon an Instutute*
someone dared to ask
where in this damn building
do they hide the masks?

many in their closets
others in the baths
maybe on the terrace?
(where Bongs* prepared, amass)

Palladio* 'til dawn
visions roust about
(beyond the building made of
books*)
a hamburger cries out

within McDonalds* swarms survive
a spectacle in sight
creatures here of every stripe
imagining the night

((🔔)) Time

....the projects to whack-up:

♪ a   b c d e f   g
"splayed about before the masks
  h i j k (l m n) o p
  salivate before repasts"

—

* Institute for Architecture and
Urban Studies

* study models of architecture
projects

* Andrea Palladio "The Four Books
of Architecture"

* The New York Public Library

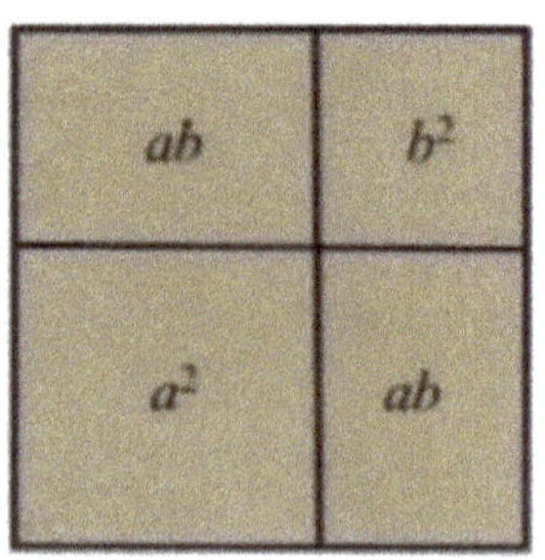

ab
b²
a²
ab

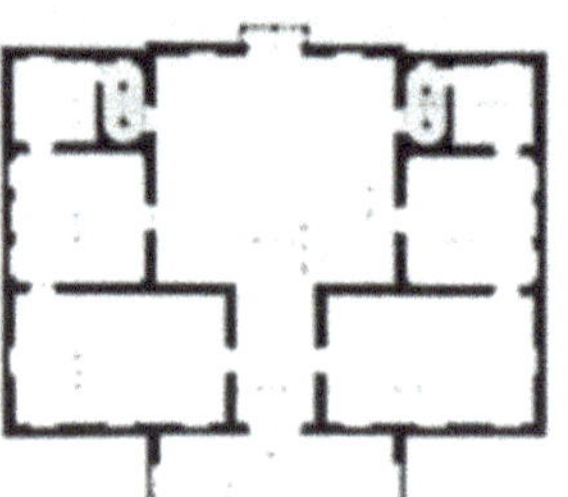

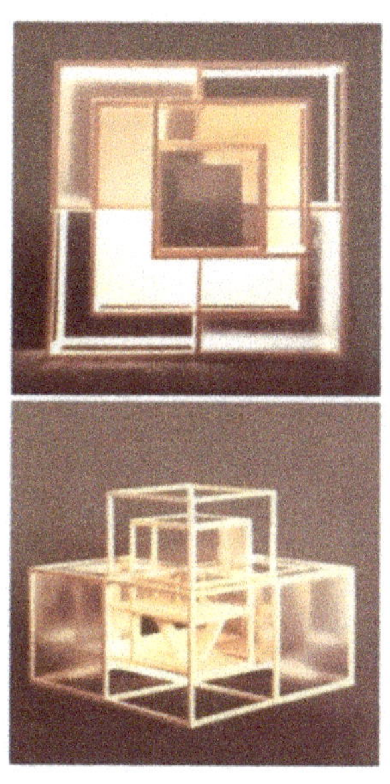

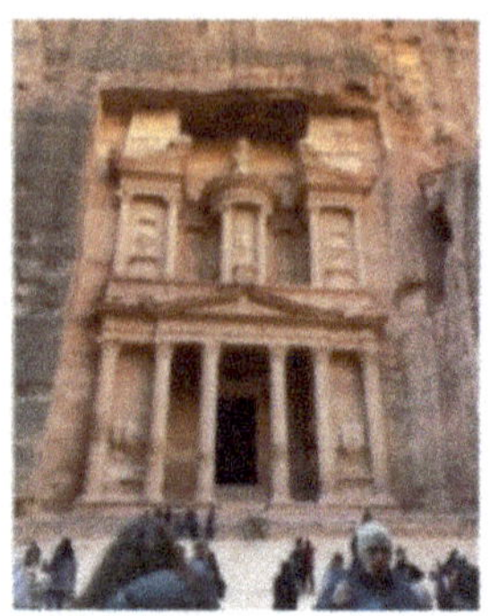

In a Petran Tomb

    a poet reclines
    moist
    and rank
    on a couch of 🌈 stone

    scent of earth
    drops to quench
    souls from ancient seas

    wretched creatures
    imagined dwelling

    in a Petran Tomb

Copernicus
displaced the earth
and centered the sun

Galileo
initiated hypotheses
that required proof

Newton
explained that what happened
speaks in mathematics

Freud
conjured dreams
to interpret them

Einstein
observed objects
revealing relativity

Archimedes confirmed
that the distance around your waist
divided by
the distance across your waist
= "pi" (an irrational number)

📓 Pocket Quintets

a little girl played music
on a grand piano
her little sister
grabbed her hair
and pulled her off the chair

a big baby boy waits
to bully
his brother
while parents drink
downstairs after six

a trusting child
dragged to school
lay on the floor
and kicked the door
without shoes

aqua cream tables
and pineapple juice
with chatter
and social teas
teach etiquette

against a wall
an upright
pounds sounds
to march to
around in circles

blocks piled high
without form
balanced with care
crashed by a boy
while worlds were at war

what rhymes with candy
andy
andy done
first friend
friend for life

clubs and pranks
secrets shared
safe in the shade
of a forsythia bush
in full spring bloom

grim
brothers of fairy tales
she hansel
me gretel sing
if at night we were to sleep

oh say have you sung
from a choir stall
facing people
in the town
you live in

there was crime
required to join
whatever gang
opposed society
and guilt

music theory
picture a sidewalk inclined
outside a picture window
legs longer shorter shorter longer
strolling by

summer camp
with horses
and french teachers
and good conduct pins
for cooperation

someone had an idea
to skate in pain
and progress with tests
while others
preferred seven layer cake

back in the garden of kinder
gretel knew
the story required
the annihilation
of witches

which suggests
bitches
flocks of a feather
fitting together
flying

friends become frenemies
frenemies friends
that all is not fair
in strife or life
smarts

medals of silver
medals of gold
trophies to hold
for jumping and spinning
on very thin ice

bursts of ballet
arms aflutter
legs maneuvering
leveraged like levers
into positions like cranes

upper west
college collage
where gentlemen
called barnard
barnyard

job of jobs
teach nice girls
to write and read
venn diagrams
in first grade

boy oh joy a baby boy
to love and feed
to rock and to coo to
and sing to too
to lullaby to sleep

amadeus
âme de dieu
whose stars twinkle
a je vous dirais
maman

good night moon
aesops fables
do not run away bunny
books by seuss
and a doctor named spock

joy oh boy another boy
his brothers turf to tread
cars and trucks
and trains with names
trying on various hats

time to cool
thoughts respool
reach for something new
back to school
brain retool

weird projects
designing interiors
visual concepts on fry days
critique after two
after daiquiris

scheidungskrise
saddest days
do not look back
at psychic pain
live tomorrow today

zu hilfe zu hilfe
bin ich veloren
der schlage zum opfer
erkoren
ach rettet mich

hours of riches
probing a mind
distressed
repressed
yet blest

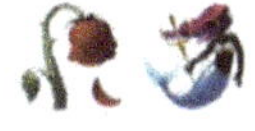

with hope beyond words
I have loved

crushed in time

in meaning
beyond words

                    time is now
                to begin beyond

                a time long ago

                beyond beyond
            for love of ones own

what
is architecture
with a capital a
or building with a little b
a bb c bb a

nine square grids
palladian plans
transformations
reconfigured in variations
like figure skating programs

theater of kinds
of theories of minds
who has a mind
or not
knows not

what is absurd
is not absurd
entertainment
to a crowd
of participants

piercing arts
colorful
skin graffiti
billboards
plus ornaments

ones
unforgivable
those loved
hoped would love me
forever

painful experience
poetically expressed
as grapefruits squeezed
with unwashed rinds
digested

when again
to begin again
in youth or middle age
or last of days
with best to say

afterlives
live in lyrics
embedded
in songs
enstoned

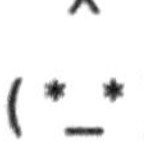

Radishes

I know you know
you know I know

if he loves she
and she loves he
or they love they
and they love he
or he loves they
and they love me
who are they
who love?

if all we need is love
and who knows
knows what love is
who cares what Peter Rabbit ate

Quote for today

"The focus of subjectivity is a
distorting mirror"

Hans- Georg Gadamer

Re: Quote for today

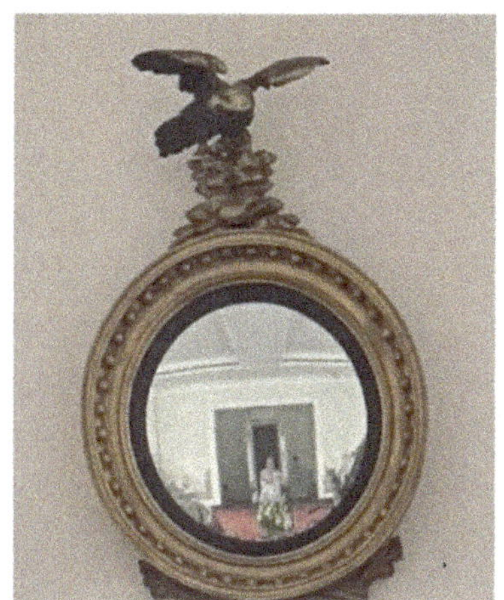

psychoanalysis
精神分析

    clouds among clouds
    adrift
    in suspension
    destined for oblivion

beyond

    words within worlds
    dreamt
    and bound
    by resistance

between

    minds intertwined
    dancing
    precariously
    on a beam of light

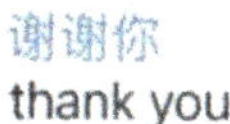

谢谢你
thank you

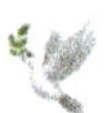
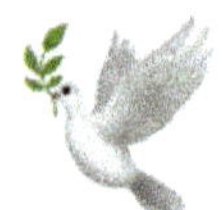
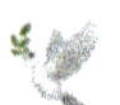